Angela Rippon's

Learn with

Victoria Plum

TREES

Purnell

Published 1985 by Purnell Books, Paulton, Bristol, BS18 5LQ,
a member of the BPCC group.
Made and printed by Purnell and Sons (Book Production) Limited, Paulton, Bristol

HELLO! THIS IS ONE OF MY FAVOURITE PLACES. UNDER THIS WONDERFUL CANOPY OF TREES NEAR MY WOODLAND HOME, I FEEL THAT I'M IN A BIG AIRY ROOM WITH THE SUN PEEPING THROUGH THE LACY GREEN CURTAINS OVER MY HEAD. AND IF IT STARTS TO RAIN — WELL, THE BRANCHES WILL PROTECT ME FROM GETTING WET. TREES ARE NATURE'S LARGEST PLANTS, AND WE HAVE TO LOVE AND LOOK AFTER THEM, BECAUSE THEY MAKE THE WORLD SO BEAUTIFUL. WOULDN'T IT BE A BARE OLD PLACE WITHOUT TREES? THERE ARE MANY DIFFERENT KINDS OF TREE BUT I'VE CHOSEN JUST SOME OF THE ONES YOU CAN FIND GROWING NEAR YOU — SO THAT YOU CAN LEARN TO RECOGNISE THEM. AND WHILE YOU'RE DOING THAT YOU'LL MEET LOTS OF MY ANIMAL FRIENDS — BIRDS AND INSECTS, TOO — WHO NEED TREES TO LIVE IN. UNDER, INSIDE, ON TOP — A TREE CAN BE A HOME TO MANY LITTLE CREATURES, ALL AT THE SAME TIME! OF COURSE, I LIKE TREES — I'M A TREE FAIRY. BUT YOU WILL LIKE TREES TOO, WHEN YOU GET TO KNOW THEM. HAVE FUN WITH THIS BOOK!

It's hard to believe, but this mighty oak was once a tiny sapling, and before that an even tinier shoot.

New shoot (just emerging from the soil).

Oak sapling, about three years old.

Oak tree, fully grown.

Victoria always makes a record of what she sees on her woodland strolls. She makes little sketches and labels them as she goes. You could try this too; it's a good way to remember what you saw.

There are two kinds of trees. Some lose their leaves in wintertime, turning pretty shades of red, brown and yellow as the leaves die. They usually have broad leaves and they are called *deciduous* trees. Their seeds usually grow inside *fruit*, like nuts or apples.

Other trees, called *conifers*, are *evergreen* because they never lose their leaves, which sometimes don't look like leaves at all, but spiky needles. Their seeds are usually inside woody cones.

Although both sorts of tree may grow near each other, they are often grown separately, because the conifers grow quite fast and are planted in special forests especially for timber.

On the left is a coniferous forest of pines, and on the right is the one Victoria lives in—a deciduous forest. Different animals and plants live in each type of wood.

Parts of a tree

The *trunk* of a tree is its thick, woody stem, which is covered in *bark*. Under the bark are tubes which carry *sap*, the tree's food. If the bark is stripped off, the tubes may be damaged and the tree could die.

Bark is a bit like people's skin—it's smooth when the tree is young, but it gets cracked and wrinkled with age. That's because bark doesn't stretch, so as the tree-trunk grows the bark has to split. But the tree is always protected, because it grows a new layer of bark under the old one.

Did you know that the *roots* of a tree spread out as far as the branches do above it? The roots support the tree—especially in high winds—and supply it with enough food and water from the earth.

The *branches*, with *twigs* on them, hold the leaves up to the light. A tree needs lots of branches and twigs, so that as many leaves as possible can face the sunlight. The tree needs sunlight for making its food.

The *leaves* take in sunlight and gas from the air, which mix with mineral salts and water brought from the roots. Using a green substance in the leaves called *chlorophyll*, these make food for the tree.

When a tree has been growing for several years it *flowers*, and produces *seeds*.

Rings of age

If you have ever seen the stump of a tree which has been cut down, you'll know that it is marked with rings. These spread out from the *heartwood*, at the centre of the trunk, to the young *sapwood* near the bark. Each ring marks one growing season of the tree. So, counting one ring for every year, you can make a good guess at how old the tree was when it was cut down.

Things which are made from wood all start life as part of a tree. When the tree is cut down, the huge log is taken to the sawmill where it is cut into planks.

Conifer wood is called *softwood*, and is used a lot for building work.

Broad-leafed tree wood is called *hardwood*, and is used for furniture.

When you look at a plank of wood, you don't see tree-rings, but vertical lines running up and down the plank. This is because the plank is cut *down* the tree, not across it. You would see the same effect if you cut down through a piece of seaside rock—instead of getting the name of your holiday resort, you would get long lines of colour running up and down it.

There have been trees on Earth for many millions of years. People have always loved trees, and now we try to plant enough new ones to replace the ones we chop down.

Trees in the country

Here's an orchard. All the trees growing here produce fruit—like apples, pears and plums. There is a high hedge growing all round the orchard to keep the cold winds out—and the fence is made from trees, too, but not fruit trees.

Some trees grow with lots of others, in woods or forests. Others stand by themselves in the middle of a meadow, pretending to be umbrellas for lots of lazy cows.

Some trees are grown in rows, acting as a growing fence for crops and animals. They stop the wind from making the air very cold.

On steep hillsides, trees are planted to stop the soil from rolling down to the bottom. The tree roots bind together the soil so that crops can grow.

Trees you might see in the country:—

Oak You'll recognise the fruit of this tree — the acorn!

Ash This tree has pretty pale grey bark.

Horse Chestnut The conker tree.

Beech Beech nuts are a triangle shape. They grow inside brown husks.

Never damage any trees that you see growing, because you will be spoiling the landscape for everyone else. If you go on a picnic in the country try to leave it as you found it. And *never* carve your initials on a tree—it may seem a small mark to make but it could be dangerous for the tree.

Trees in the town

People in towns can enjoy trees, too! Victoria knows this, because she often visits her cousin, the Smoke Fairy, who lives right in the middle of a big city.

Poplar Tree
London Plane
Horse Chestnut
Silver Birch
Common Lime
Sycamore
"Some of our streets are called avenues, and have trees growing along the pavements...
...and some shopping centres have trees growing around, with seats in between them for tired shoppers...
...and there are trees in school grounds...
... just look around!"

Tree homes up high . . .

A *squirrel's* home is called a *drey*. This is a grey squirrel, and it eats all sort of things, like nuts, buds and bark from the trees among which it lives, also bulbs and toadstools.

Down the trunk a little way a *woodpecker* is busily making itself a new home. It does this by tapping out a hole in the trunk of the tree. The family's eggs are laid and hatched inside the hole. Food is found in the tree too—woodpeckers hear the sound of small insects under the bark and probe behind to catch the insects, with their long beaks and tongues.

The *robin* will make its home anywhere, but a favourite spot is in a broad-leaved tree such as an oak. It's known as a jolly little bird, but it will fight anyone who tries to come on to its territory!

The *tawny owl* roosts in the fork of a tree in the daytime, and hunts at night. It makes its nest in a treehole, too. It waits and watches patiently up in the branches until it sees some food to catch.

An old woodpecker hole makes a good nest for a *nuthatch*, a little bird which is very clever at climbing. It can walk down tree-trunks headfirst! The tree provides food as well as a home for the nuthatch, because the little bird eats tiny caterpillars it finds in the trunk.

. . . and down low!

Wood ants usually live in pine forests, and they use pine needles to make their nests. The mound which is the nest can be as much as a metre high, with an old tree stump as a base. Worker ants go out from this huge home in vast armies to catch greenfly, which they then milk for their honeydew. The greenfly are not harmed; but it's another story for the caterpillars, which the ants take back to the nest as food.

The rabbit's enemy, the *fox*, lives in a burrow called an *earth*, usually under a tree root, although it's sometimes in a bank. Rabbits often spoil trees by eating the bark, but the fox eats the rabbits instead of the trees—which is better for the trees but hard on the rabbits!

The *badger* may make its home, called a *set*, under a tree root. It will probably use the same set as its parents and grandparents used. Dried leaves from the trees above cover the floor, although they are regularly turned out and replaced with new ones.

The *bank vole* likes to nest in decaying tree stumps, and is very fond of chewing tree bark. It can climb well and may make a meal of high branches as well as low!

Make a tree notebook

Things to write down:

When leaves fall from the branches—or buds form and open into new leaves in spring.

The animals you see in the tree at different times of the year.

Birds which nest in the tree.

Insects on the tree at different times of the year.

Plants growing on or around the tree.

Don't study too large an area at first, or you could soon get fed up. Draw a little map, and mark each tree on it in green. Mark houses and other buildings in red.

If there are too many trees all at once—in a wood, for instance—shade in the whole area in green, write 'Many trees here', and concentrate on others which appear singly.

You may not know the name of each tree. Get out a good guide book to trees from your library, and see if you can identify them. If you're not sure, ask someone to help you.

Other things to write down:
Which trees are the biggest.
The measurement round the trunk at the height of your knees and shoulders.
When the trees flower and fruit.

Whichever sort of study you choose to do, it will look much better with pictures in it. Draw these pictures yourself, and take photos too sometimes, so that you can compare the scene in summer with the same place in winter.

You can stick leaves from the trees in, and drawings of the fruit—acorns, pine cones, whatever; if it is a horse chestnut tree you could record battles fought with its conkers!

Trees are useful

When trees are cut down their wood makes many things.

They are used for making houses . . .

and for the furniture we put inside them . . .

and for making paper . . .

and boats . . . and cricket bats . . . and all sorts of things!

Look around your home and see just how many things there are which are wooden.

How many wooden objects can you spot in Victoria's house?

In many parts of the world there are trees which can help us while they are still growing.

Maple syrup is taken from trees.

Rubber is made from special trees in South America and Asia. It's used for car tyres, foam rubber, balls and balloons for children to play with . . . and lots, lots more.

Gum comes from the eucalyptus tree to make floor polish, paint, varnish, crayons, perfume and soap.

A different type of gum, from the sapodilla tree, makes chewing gum!

Then there is all the fruit we eat— oranges, pears, apples, plums, peaches, cherries— that keeps us healthy.

Let's think of trees as big friends . . . and treat them with loving respect. If you would like to know more about trees, look for some books in your local library, and write (enclosing a stamped addressed envelope) to:

The Forestry Commission,
231 Corstorphine Road,
Edinburgh,
Scotland.

They will send you, if you ask them to, a list of their forest parks, where you can camp and picnic among beautiful scenery. They have also planned out some interesting nature trails, and have pamphlets on trees and wildlife.